WE CALL THIS H•ME

Published by We Call This Home LLC
www.wecallthishome.com

Cover : Roy Hobbs
Editor: Alec Liu
Layout: Johnathan Min

ISBN: 978-0-9765496-3-5

First Edition: March 2016

Printed in South Korea

For my parents, who left everything behind and traveled half way around the world to find a new home.

WE CALL THIS
H●ME

PREFACE

I was a product of the '90s. The rise of pop music and the World Wide Web. Back then, the American Dream was alive and kickin', or at the very least, that's what we chose to believe and the roadmap for reaching the land of milk and honey still sheepishly straightforward. Go to college. Get a job. Live happily ever after.

I grew up in an Asian household so there was a lot of box checking, and with that comes this expectation of a payoff at the end of it all. The reality of course is that life is never quite that easy. It's also not how living a fulfilling life works, where you're constantly focused on some fruitful end-game, the culmination of a grandiose plan.

When I told my friends and family that I was going to essentially quit that life and travel around the world with no real plan, they thought I was crazy, but deep down, I knew it was something I had to do. The formula I had applied to my entire existence up to that point wasn't working. It's funny how that works, where the best decision I could ever make defied all logic. I couldn't explain to them why this was what I had to do. But something about it just felt right — even if I had no clue where any of this would lead me.

Ironically, that ended up being the best lesson I ever learned. I learned to live in the present. I can only describe this as one of the most empowering things I've ever felt. In doing so, I've been able to better appreciate my friends and family in ways that I could never have imagined. It unleashed my capacity to love.

And as my anxiety disappeared, so did a sense of guilt and most importantly, feelings of fear. Suddenly, I was chill just being me without worrying about abstract concepts of success and other people's perceptions of my decisions. The less I focused on success, the more objectively successful I felt and became. Once, I had been nothing more than a resume. The result of my three years of traveling around the world is that I became a person. And as a warm-blooded human being, I've finally learned to enjoy life and the journey that ultimately defines who we really are.

In sharing my story, I can only hope that it will engender a bit of confidence for anyone out there, who, like me, was debating whether or not to take that leap into the rabbit hole and maybe cross off some items from that bucket list we all have. Maybe that's asking a bit much. At the very least, I hope you enjoy the photos.

This book follows my travels in chronological order. The dates in the bottom margin signal the date I arrived in the corresponding country. You'll notice some significant time gaps between dates. These intervals were for extended stays in South Korea or because I returned home due to either personal reasons or for incidents out of my control, ie., getting robbed.

WE CALL THIS H ME

As a child, I was enthralled by movies, an art form with the capacity to instantly transport me to another world. At some point, I decided that I too wanted to tell stories with moving images. My dad's old camcorder in hand, I rounded up my friends and shot my first flick. By then, I was in 9th grade. And with that film, I'd apply to New York University's Tisch School of the Arts. To my great surprise and endless glee, they accepted me. I was on my way to a fulfilling life—or so I thought.

The year I graduated was the same year the global economy decided to collapse. The financial crisis of 2008 would be the worst since the Great Depression. Suddenly, all the loans I'd taken out to pay for that small piece of paper with my diploma printed on it seemed like a cruel joke. Far from chasing dreams, the primary prerogative now was survival — which for me, meant not having to endure the failure symbolized by having to move back in with my parents.

So instead of pursuing the lifelong dream I'd attended college for in the first place, I ended up playing it safe with a full-time job as an A/V technician. I rationalized that this was some temporary detour. I was still pursuing my dreams, I told myself. This was just to hold me over until the economy improved. And just like that, three years went by. To make matters worse, it was a grueling job often requiring 60-80 hours a week, many times at odd hours. When you're in the event production business, you're usually working when other people are having fun.

> " I rationalized that this was some temporary detour. I was still pursuing my dreams, I told myself. This was just to hold me over until the economy improved. And just like that, three years went by. "

I felt completely lost. With no clear exit strategy, the only thing I felt I necessary was to start saving every penny I earned. If I've never been the most courageous liver of life, I've been lucky enough to have a sense of discipline, which I owe to my immigrant parents. Consequently, by 2010, my general purpose nest egg had reached a comfortable size. I didn't yet have a plan, but during the grind of work, I often found myself daydreaming of seeing the world, maybe doing some light traveling. It was all very basic. Ask anyone and "travel more" is one of their New Year's resolutions.

The difference for me, was that, for the first time in my life, my bank account was relatively flush after years of being the guy who lives in New York and never parties. I knew I could quit my job and be okay for a while. That's when I started planning a trip to Southeast Asia. What started as a three-month getaway would eventually balloon into a year-long break. I'd only traveled beyond American borders twice in my life—trips to the Bahamas and later Paris. In a sense, I was totally clueless, your typical uncultured suburbanite.

As my travel ambitions grew, I realized I'd need to live even more frugally. By then, I was totally committed. Rent in New York is sort of atrocious so I moved out of my apartment, sold most of my belongings, and started sleeping on the couches of friends. They thought I'd lost my mind, but I guess they were trying to be polite. After a while, I started to feel bad so I brought a sleeping bag to work and slept in the projection booth of our building's theater. I made sure to wake up before workers arrived and showered at the gym. I had been taking finance and economics classes at Columbia on the side. I was still an investing novice but I decided to park some cash in the stock market. Everything had just crashed so I figured there was only one way things could go. That was the hope anyway. Call it beginner's luck, but those initial investments would allow me to extend my trip some more.

Then on September 21, 2011, I got on a plane.

JAPAN

The gods decided to test my fortitude immediately. In Japan, my first stop, my passport wallet must have fallen out of my bag while on a bus in Kyoto, with it my Chinese visa and around $300 in cash.

At that point, I was still putting outsized blame on myself for impossible to foresee potholes. Which meant I was devastated. How could I be so stupid? I had literally just started. Inevitable doubts crept into every thought. Was I cut out for this?

> **"Inevitable doubts crept into every thought. Was I cut out for this?"**

For four days, I basically existed in limbo, unsure whether to go on or call it quits. On the fifth day, I decided that this sexy life as a world traveler didn't suit me and headed to the US embassy so I could get an emergency passport and head home. What was I thinking anyway? I get to the embassy and fill out all the forms and explain my story to the embassy employee. As I'm about to pay, he stops me. Wait, you've come all this way. Let's check with the police one last time, he suggests. At this point, I'm already so resigned to the fact that I've messed everything up that this suggestion actually annoys me. Seriously? Waste more time with false hope? I reluctantly agree, mostly out of conditioned politeness.

As it happens, that last minute call saved me. The police had my wallet. My wallet was as I had left it, except for the $300. That had been moved to a different pocket. Only in Japan.

ABOVE:

Floating Torii - Itsukushima Shrine - Miyajima Island

RIGHT:

Gion District - Tokyo

献立

おまかせ

京の晩ごはん

五、八〇〇円

祇園 かわ富

祇園
かわ富

ABOVE:

Tokyo's Tsukiji Fish Market is the largest wholesale seafood market in the world. Licensed buyers inspect the tuna they will bid on later during the auction.

JR Pass, handy for train travel throughout most of the country

SOUTH KOREA

South Korean Won

Gyeongbokgung Palace Ticket

CHINA

My time in China was special. It was early on in my travels and it was the first country to really take my breath away.

I'd never before encountered life so wildly different from what I was used to back home in the U.S. It was absolutely fascinating.

Yet despite my often remote location, I regularly ran into other backpackers along the way. This was a thing, it dawned on me.

> **I assumed that what I was doing was relatively unique, at least that's what it felt like among my friends.**

During my preparation, I didn't read that many blogs. I assumed that what I was doing was relatively unique, at least that's what it felt like among my friends. In fact, countless people were doing the exact same thing and many had been traveling for just as long as I had planned for, if not longer. It was here in China that I made the decision to continue backpacking until I was totally sick of it or dead broke, whichever came first.

Chinese Yuan Renminbi

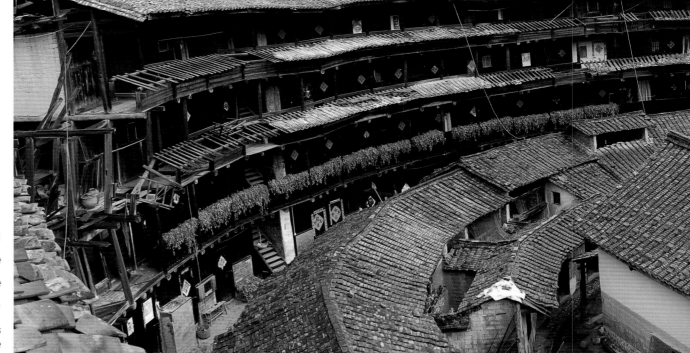

OPPOSITE PAGE, TOP ROW, FROM LEFT:

Pingyao - Shanxi Province

Dazhai Rice Terraces - Guangxi Province

BOTTOM:

Hakka Tolou in Yongding District of Longyan. This is the tolou I slept overnight in. Bathrooms came in the form of a bucket just outside the room.

TOP ROW, FROM LEFT TO RIGHT:

Dongchuan Red Soil - Yunnan Province

BOTTOM ROW, FROM LEFT TO RIGHT:

Xingping - Guangxi Province

Dongchuan Red Soil - Yunnan Province

FULL SPREAD:

The sea of motorbikes in Ho Chi Minh City

CLOCKWISE, FROM TOP LEFT:

Pineapple Vendor - Mekong Delta

Ho Chi Minh City

Tam Coc - Ninh Binh Province

LEFT & CENTER:

Phnom Penh

RIGHT & OPPOSITE PAGE:

Ta Prohm - Angkor Wat Archaeological Park

Bayon - Angkor Wat Archaeological Park

15

Cambodian Riel

THAILAND

CLOCKWISE, FROM LEFT:

White Temple - Chiang Rai

Rai Leh - Krabi Province

Lottery Ticket Vendor - Chiang Mai

FULL SPREAD:

Ko Lanta - Krabi Province

FROM TOP TO BOTTOM:

Plain of Jars - Phonsovan

Kuang Si Falls - Luang Prabang

OPPOSITE PAGE, FROM LEFT TO RIGHT:

Monks Collecting Alms - Luang Prabang

Luang Prabang

Laotian Kip

NEPAL

Seven days. That's how long it took by foot to make it to Everest Base Camp and to the top of Kala Patthar, a viewpoint overlooking base camp. Three hours. That's the most, prior to this trek, that I'd ever hiked in one go.

That experience changed me. To walk in the endless shadows of these snow capped giants was so humbling, like walking among gods. You feel so puny and insignificant. You're disconnected.

> " **To walk in the endless shadows of these snow capped giants was so humbling, like walking among gods.** "

And that quiet solitude along with the realization that you don't really matter is a profound feeling — a stark contrast to the furious bustle of life in the Concrete Jungle. From there on out, trekking would become a priority when mapping out my travel plans.

Nepalese Rupee

RIGHT:

Nepalese Royal Guard - Kathmandu

Entrance Permit for Everest Base Camp Trek

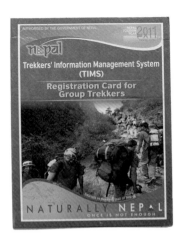

TIMS card for Trekking in Nepal

RIGHT:

Everest Base Camp Treck Trail

BELOW:

View from Kala Patthar with Mount Everest in background

TOP LEFT & RIGHT:

We didn't travel alone. We were accompanied by Nepalese porters who easily outpaced us while carrying their own weight in goods meant for distant villages.

OPPOSITE PAGE & BOTTOM LEFT:

Namche Bazaar - Khumbu Region

I can only describe Varanasi as a pounding headache. The sights, smells, and sounds can at times be physically overwhelming.

As one of the oldest cities in the world and the holiest destination for Hindus, the city's vibrant history is accompanied by a palpable energy.

> ## A walk down the river path is a story of life and death.

People and cows, cars and bicycles jockey for position on the tightly packed streets without working traffic lights. A walk down the river path is a story of life and death. Thousands bathe in the Ganges River each morning and wash their clothes, downstream from where their dearest departed are cremated daily.

ABOVE & FULL SPREAD:

Varanasi - Uttar Pradesh

Indian Rupee

LEFT & TOP RIGHT:

Jodhpur - Rajasthan

BOTTOM RIGHT & OPPOSITE PAGE:

At any time, over 100,000 people are gathered in worship at the Golden Temple in Amritsar, the holy place of Sikhs, where free meals are provided daily by a volunteer run kitchen. Foreigners are free to spend the night in dormitories inside the temple grounds while other visitors camp out in the various courtyards. Even amid the energy of overwhelming crowds, there exists a deep sense of tranquility.

LEFT:

Jaipur Fort - Jaipur - Rajasthan

RIGHT:

Abhaneri - Rajasthan

OPPOSITE PAGE:

Srinagar - Kashmir Valley

Taj Mahal Ticket - Agra - Rajasthan

TURKEY

Turkish Lira

LEFT:

Galata Bridge - Istanbul

RIGHT:

Grand Bazaar - Istanbul

OPPOSITE PAGE:

Cappadocia - Central Anatolia

Turkey

GREECE

LEFT:

Heraklion - Crete

RIGHT & OPPOSITE PAGE:

Santorini Island

EGYPT

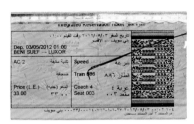

FROM TOP TO BOTTOM:

Great Temple of Ramesses II - Abu Simbel - Nubia Region

White Desert National Park - Farafa Depression

CENTER:

Cairo

ABOVE:

Nearby Tahrir Square - Cairo

36

JORDAN

Jordanian Dinar

Ticket to Petra

BELOW:

Dead Sea Jordanian Side

FULL SPREAD:

Wadi Rum Desert

Israeli Shekel

OPPOSITE PAGE, FROM LEFT TO RIGHT:

The Treasury - Petra - Ma'an Governate

The Siq - Petra - Ma'an Governate

LEFT:

Old City - Jerusalem

RIGHT:

Wailing Wall - Old City - Jerusalem

USA

TOP:

Golden Gate Bridge - San Francisco - California

BOTTOM LEFT:

Las Vegas - Nevada

My footwear of choice

BOTTOM RIGHT:

Scheduling around my brother's graduation, I found myself stateside at the Roost in Bellingham, Washington to catch up with Jonah and Greg, friends I made in Vietnam. When my sandals broke while visiting Halong Bay, Greg spared me his sandals, pictured above. They became my footwear of choice for the remainder of my travels, repaired by cobblers in four different regions of the world, stepping into just over 60 countries.

OPPOSITE PAGE:

Great Sand Dunes National Park - Colorado

NORTH KOREA

As a Korean American, North Korea was the motherland that wasn't. It's surreal to think that, not fifty years ago, these people were my brothers and sisters, living under one flag.

In the presence of tourists, North Koreans possess a visible shyness, a sense of caution. I did, however, chat up my tour guide, Mr. Lee. Respect of elders is deeply embedded in Korean culture. As we bonded over shots of soju, Korea's liquor of choice, both North and South, Mr. Lee began treating me like a younger brother, a sign of affection.

> **When you strip away the war and the politics, we're all people with families and hopes and dreams, human beings trying to survive another day.**

We shared stories about our families, my life growing up in America. I was taken aback at how easily we found common ground. When you strip away the war and the politics, we're all people with families and hopes and dreams, human beings trying to survive another day.

Pyongyang Metro Ticket

Postcards from a tourist giftshop

RIGHT:

Kaeson Youth Park - Pyongyang

OPPOSITE PAGE, TOP & BOTTOM LEFT:

Locals gather at the Pyongyang metro, one of the deepest subway systems in the world, to read and discuss the daily news. Newspapers must be carefully disposed of by special handlers since it's illegal to throw away, deface or mistreat images of party leaders.

OPPOSITE PAGE, RIGHT:

Street Life in Pyongyang

North Korea Tourist Card

North Korean Won

STARTING OPPOSITE PAGE, FROM LEFT TO RIGHT:

Street life in Pyongyang

TOP, BOTTOM & FULL SPREAD:

North Korea's Arirang Festival. It's an annual exhibition of gymnastics and arts known as the Mass Games featuring a giant, human LCD screen — the pixels represented by thousands of school children holding up posters, flickering on and off in harmonious tandem in honor of the supreme leader. Is there a better metaphor for Kim Jung-Un's totalitarian regime?

MYANMAR

Tourism in Myanmar remains underdeveloped relative to its Southeast Asian neighbors given its oppressive military government. Civil war continues in remote pockets of the country. But these hurdles only make it a more compelling destination, providing travelers a lens into the past, a relic of what tourism was like in the region twenty years ago before it went "mainstream."

There were still no functioning ATMs when I visited in 2012. Instead, cash was exchanged on the street, easy pickings for scammers and thieves targeting foreign travelers like myself. Smelling blood, local dealers quickly converged on me. I thought I had been careful. In the intense bustle of the transaction, I saw two men running the other way, but it was too late. Counting my cash, I was $300 short.

In my mind, I'd already written the loss off. It seemed hopeless, but some passers-by who spoke English stopped by to help. Frantic discussion erupted as they talked to some street vendors who had seen what happened. Then, one of the men picked up an iron bar, and we went up to the nearby apartment buildings and started banging on all the doors. We came back empty handed, but to my surprise, they didn't give up.

There was a buzz of excitement around this whole crazy ordeal and soon, random strangers started tagging along. Before long the group had swelled to well over 20 people.

> " Then, one of the men picked up an iron bar, and we went up to the nearby apartment buildings and started banging on all the doors. "

The next stop was the police station, which was closed. Instead, we located some officers drinking tea nearby. One of the policeman was familiar with the local families, and against all odds, somehow apprehended a woman associated with one of the alleged bandits, who they began interrogating aggressively on the street. During the heat of the discussion, another officer broke through the crowd, raised his hand, and slapped her with everything he had. I was shocked, at a complete loss.

The slap proved persuasive. We walked back, mob in tow, to the police station, which frankly, was nothing more than a shack. They handed the woman a phone. You could hear crying in the background—and then, without warning, the sky opened up and dropped the wettest, heaviest rain I've ever experienced. A few minutes later, a man emerged from the waterfall now covering the door and handed me $300.

The two English speaking locals who had helped me from the start suggest to me that it would be a nice gesture to offer the policemen some money for helping out—I'd also been warned about corrupt cops in Myanmar. But when I offered the officers a tip, they fervently refused. The other locals turned down my offer to take them out for dinner. Instead, they were simply relieved I wouldn't think badly of their country.

FULL SPREAD:

U Bein Bridge - Taungthaman Lake - Amarapura

TOP ROW:

Circular Train - Yangon

BOTTOM:

Bagan - Mandalay Region

OPPOSITE PAGE:

Kyaiktiyo - Mon State

Yangon Circular Train Ticket

MYANMAR

MALAYSIA

Malaysian Ringgit

CLOCKWISE, FROM TOP RIGHT:

As Syakirin Mosque - Kuala Lumpur

Malacca City - Malacca

Mabul Island - Sabah

OPPOSITE PAGE:

In Georgetown, Penang, joss paper or ghost money is used as burnt offerings for ancestors.

SINGAPORE

FROM LEFT TO RIGHT:

Marina Bay - Central Business District

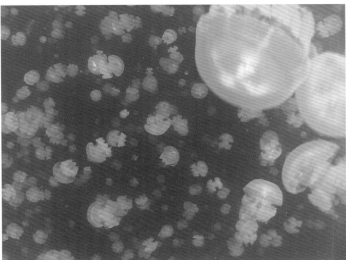

BOTTOM ROW:

A man once said—"if you don't use it, you lose it." Such is the case of Palau's jellyfish in this lake. Thousands of years without a predator have rendered their stinging cells harmless to humans.

Jellyfish Lake Ticket

PHILIPPINES

Philippine Peso

TOP & BOTTOM:

Bohol - Central Visayas Region

If eating babies is your thing, you'll love balut. Pictured here, a balut is a fertilized egg with a developing embryo, which is as about as adventurous as I got with food during my travels—although I did try cuy (guinea pig) while in Peru.

TOP RIGHT:

Cebu City - Cebu Island

LEFT:

Hanging Coffins of Sagada - Luzon Province

INDONESIA

Goa Gajah Ticket - Ubud - Bali

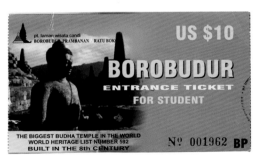

Borobudur Ticket - Central Java

FROM TOP TO BOTTOM:

Labuan Bajo - Flores

Kuta Beach - Bali

OPPOSITE PAGE:

To earn $10 a day, sulfur workers at the Ijen Crater located in East Java carry up to 100 kilos of sulfur 2.2 kilometers back to camp.

FROM LEFT TO RIGHT:

Beau – an American traveler who I met on a bus to Flores Island – and I were denied entry to Mount Kelimutu for being late. Earlier in my travels, I might have put my head down and turned around. But long emboldened, I didn't think twice about potentially breaking the rules in search of adventure off the beaten path. Turned away at the main entrance, we forged into thick shrubbery, scaling a mountain of trash, and ultimately circumvened the gate. A short hike later, we found the colored lakes, shimmering under the stars, a unique experience reserved only for audacious rule breakers.

There are three colored lakes that change color periodically, chemical reactions catalyzed by volcanic activity.

OPPOSITE PAGE:

Water Castle - Yogyakarta

Komodo NP Entrance Ticket

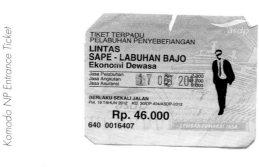

Ferry to Labuan Bajo - Flores Island

When we asked for the official bus ticket the man at the hotel reception made one up on the spot

AUSTRALIA

Uluru-Kata Tjuta NP Ticket

FROM TOP TO BOTTOM:

Manly Beach - Sydney - New South Wales

Blue Mountains - New South Wales

By feet, by bus, by train. It doesn't really matter after a while. On the way to Ayer's Rock in the Northern Territory, I hitched a ride in a garbage truck.

FULL SPREAD:

Twelve Apostles - Great Ocean Road - Victoria

New Zealand Dollar

ABOVE:

Abel Tasman NP - Nelson Tasman Region

FULL SPREAD:

Milford Sound - Fiordland NP - Southland Region

New Zealand

New Zealand

STARTING OPPOSITE PAGE, FROM LEFT TO RIGHT:

Fox Glacier - Westland Tai Poutini NP

Between Queenstown and Glenorchy - Otago Region

Lake Tekapo - Mackenzie County

PREVIOUS PAGES, FROM LEFT TO RIGHT:

Lake Marian - Fiordland NP - Southland Region

Abel Tasman NP - Nelson Tasman Region

ALASKA, USA

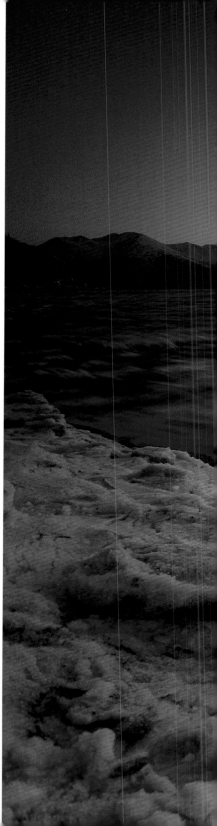

ABOVE:

Preparing the dogs for sledding in Fairbanks. The lack of sunlight during Alaska's winter really messes with your internal clock.

TOP, BOTTOM RIGHT & FULL SPREAD:

Anchorage

COLOMBIA

CLOCKWISE, FROM LEFT:

Cartagena - Caribbean Coast Region

Valle de Cocora - Los Nevados NP - Quindío

Guatapé - Antioquia Department

FROM LEFT TO RIGHT:

Outside Quito stands this equatorial monument, finished in 1982. A shame the equator is actually 240 meters north of this spot. Whoops!

Quito - Pichincha Province

BOLIVIA

Bus Ticket in Bolivia

TOP:

Lake Titicaca

BOTTOM & FULL SPREAD:

Salar de Uyuni - Potosi Department

CHILE

One of my favorite regions throughout my travels was easily South America, a mesmerizing mix of culture, sights, and breathtaking experiences. From lounging on the beaches of Rio to successfully trekking through Patagonia.

By the time I reached Calama in Chile, I had about a dozen or so photos among thousands I'd taken in South America that I felt truly proud of—the hysteria of Carnival, the grandeur of Easter Island's Maoi statues. I was certain that this was my best work yet. That's when I fell for the oldest trick in the book. While waiting for a connecting bus to San Pedro de Atacama, a man approached a friend and I, babbling nonsense. It was only ten seconds, tops, but by the time I turned around, my bag was already gone. I had lost everything.

> " It was only ten seconds, tops, but by the time I turned around, my bag was already gone. I had lost everything. "

My equipment was insured but the photos and videos were irreplaceable. There are few times in my life that I've felt so lost, depressed even. To work so hard, to feel so proud, and then suddenly, just like that, to have nothing to show for it. How was this fair? That experience in Chile proved to be a formative experience. It forced me to grow.

For one, I learned my lesson. For instance, these days, I keep my backups of essential photos on the cloud. But more importantly, that loss pushed me to overcome. I had no other choice. I couldn't simply give up. If the photographs I captured were so great, I had to prove that I could take them again, perhaps even better ones.

And so I persevered. In a way, losing my most cherished moments from my trip was the best thing that could have happened, allowing me to go further than I could have ever imagined.

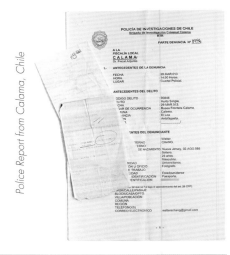

Police Report from Calama, Chile

ABOVE:

Moai Statues at Sunrise - Easter Island

Several photos taken by my friend Tom are the only images that remain from those 1.5 months of travel.

Mexican Peso

Entrance Ticket to Chichen Itza

ABOVE:

Chichen Itza - Yucatán

TOP & BOTTOM RIGHT:

An impromptu feast with some local fisherman on Isla Holbox, Quintana Roo.

Cuban Moneda Nacional

FROM LEFT TO RIGHT & FULL SPREAD:

Havana

Without Internet, it's all about the streets, which in Cuba, are bubbling with life at all times of day—the gossipy chatter of neighbors, the innocent shrill of children playing cap ball, or the pitter patter of an impromptu rain shower.

ABOVE:

Cards issued by ETECSA – internet cafes owned by the government and one of the limited ways to access the internet in Cuba. The only problem is that they're far too expensive for the average Cuban, though this may change given recent developments in U.S.- Cuban relations.

STARTING OPPOSITE PAGE, FROM LEFT TO RIGHT:

Cienfuegos

Havana

Trinidad

NAMIBIA

Shortly after getting all my stuff stolen, I almost died. Two hours outside the city limits of Windhoek, Namibia, surrounded by vast empty plains, I suddenly lost control of my vehicle on the abandoned dirt road. As the car barrel-rolled onto its side, I blacked out.

When I regained consciousness, I was covered in glass, but thankfully, right side up. Stumbling out of the car, I checked myself for injuries, staring at the smashed car in shock. Somehow I had escaped with nothing but a slight bump on my head. The remnants of the groceries I had packed for the trip surrounded the crash site, completely obliterated. That could have been me, I thought. My legs started to wobble, forcing me to sit down.

I simply sat there, doing nothing in particular besides soak in the magnitude of what had just happened. Having my stuff stolen was one thing, but nearly dying alone in the desert was a level I wasn't prepared for. Physically and emotionally exhausted, I threw in the towel. It was time to go home.

" **Why not? It's not like it could get any worse. Despite nearly being a hyena's dinner, I decided to go with the flow.** "

After waiting on the side of the road for nearly an hour, a family of three pulled over and lent me their phone. I called the rental car company to explain the accident. Without really listening to me, the representative assured me another car was on the way. I tried to correct her. I didn't want another car. I wanted to get out of here. But then something weird happened and a sense of calm took over. Why not? It's not like it could get any worse. Life wanted to keep taking wild swings at me but I couldn't let these setbacks dictate my future. Despite nearly being a hyena's dinner, I decided to go with the flow.

OPPOSITE PAGE, CLOCKWISE, FROM TOP LEFT :

Deadvlei - Sossusvlei - Namib-Naukluft National Park

Namib-Naukluft National Park

Climbing Dune 45 - Namib-Naukluft National Park

Namibian Dollar

Air Namibia Boarding Pass

BELOW:

Etosha National Park

OPPOSITE PAGE, TOP LEFT:

Namib-Naukluft National Park

OPPOSITE PAGE, RIGHT & BOTTOM LEFT:

Etosha National Park

ZIMBABWE

FROM LEFT TO RIGHT:

Victoria Falls Zimbabwean side

Victoria Falls Zambia side

FULL SPREAD:

Mana Pools National Park

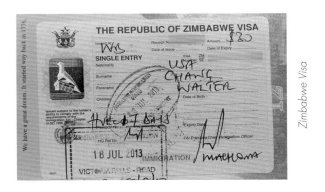

Zimbabwe Visa

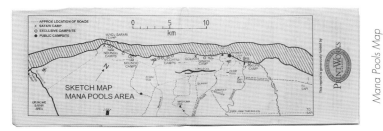

Mana Pools Map

The weird thing about beauty is that it never has to be explained to you. You just know. That's what I felt at Mana Pools National Park. The 70 km of dirt road that connects the park to civilization is notoriously bad, deterring casual passengers. The result is a refreshingly crowd-free safari.

The park is completely open. There aren't any fences, even at campsites, where visitors are even allowed to get out of their cars, if they're brave enough. Baboons scurry, play and howl, along with hippos, bathing and socializing in the Zambezi River, unfettered by the packs of hyenas on the prowl. As the sun begins to set, lions emerge, a powerful mother commanding her pride.

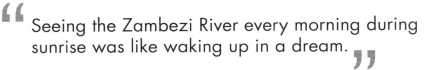

"
Seeing the Zambezi River every morning during sunrise was like waking up in a dream. "

This is the jungle, of which you are a voyeur. It's a truly magical experience, such as the candid innocence of having an elephant walk straight towards you during a mid-afternoon break. Lounging in a lawn chair, I counted the steps as the majestic animal approached until it was only an arm's length away.

Seeing the Zambezi River every morning during sunrise was like waking up in a dream.

LEFT & OPPOSITE PAGE:

Mana Pools National Park

RIGHT:

What can ten trillion dollars buy you? Less than toilet paper, actually. Hyperinflation devastated Zimbabwe's economy in 2008. At its worst, as one local explained to me, a trip to the local market saw the price of juice change three times as he waited in line before the store simply shut down.

MOZAMBIQUE

Bus Ticket to Maputo

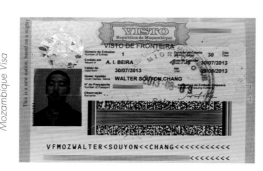

Mozambique Visa

LEFT:

Crowded minibus to Maputo

RIGHT & FULL SPREAD:

Vilankulo - Inhambane Province

NEXT PAGES, FROM LEFT TO RIGHT:

Tofo Beach - Inhambane Province

Vilankulo - Inhambane Province

Mozambique

SOUTH AFRICA

FROM TOP TO BOTTOM:

Gansbaai - Western Cape

Cape of Good Hope

OPPOSITE PAGE:

Kruger National Park – Limpopo and Mpumalanga Provinces

Childhood is full of favorites. The color blue. The number 8. Then there was the cheetah. With its speed and slender physique, it was my favorite animal as a kid. What I would have given to see one in the wild. It's rare that you ever fulfill a true childhood dream. Exiting Kruger National Park, I did just that, crossing paths with a mother and her cubs.

Basotho Loti

Minibus ticket to Maletsunyane Falls

FROM TOP TO BOTTOM & FULL SPREAD:

Semonkong - Maseru District

UNITED ARAB EMIRATES

RIGHT:

Burj Khalifa - Dubai

OPPOSITE PAGE, LEFT & RIGHT:

Nizwa - Ad Dakhiliyah

KYRGYZSTAN

Kyrgyzstani Som

CLOCKWISE, FROM TOP:

Sary Tash - Alay Valley - Osh Region

No Man's Land - Kyrgyzstan/Tajikistan Border

Hitchhiking from Bishkek to Osh

OPPOSITE PAGE:

Karakol - Issyk-Kul Province

ABOVE:

I reconnected with Beau in Kyrgyzstan. Along with Edson, a Brazilian traveler, we would join two others, Max and Sandro. We spent the next week together, traversing the Silk Road, wandering the open air museum of the Pamir Mountains.

We would all soon part our separate ways. It was only a glimmer, but our time together would leave a lasting impression. In a sense, my travels culminated to this moment. Independent souls serendipitously coming together to experience a beautiful moment in life without expectation and without fear of goodbye. This, I learned, was the essence of traveling, the soul of adventure.

FROM LEFT TO RIGHT:

Fann Mountains near Panjakent

Pamir Mountain Range

OPPOSITE PAGE:

Farmers on the Pamir Highway near Murghab

FROM LEFT TO RIGHT:

Pamir Highway near Karakul

Assisting a jeep that got stuck in the process of pulling crops out of the lake.

Homestay near Iskashim

Tajikistan Somoni

UZBEKISTAN

TOP LEFT:

The introduction of larger bills couldn't keep up with the pace of rapid inflation in Uzbekistan. The largest Som note is a 10,000 note but it's incredibly rare to come by. Same with the 5,000 note. That leaves the 1,000 note, which is roughly 20 cents in U.S. dollars. You do feel rich for a moment though.

RIGHT:

Bukhara

BOTTOM LEFT:

Samarkand

There was a time when my younger brother Ben and I were inseparable playmates. In the limited world that we knew, we were each other's best friends. But at some point, we started to grow apart.

As the oldest son in an Asian household, I felt an immense pressure to conform to my parents' expectations. The result was a teen who worked hard but was insular and socially awkward.

Ben, on the other hand, was brash with a short temper, easily miffed if he didn't get his way. He was free and easy going, making friends quickly. Four years younger, his age and attitude didn't always mesh with my immediate goals. We no longer got along. By the time I left for college, we were barely speaking.

And as adulthood beckoned, there was scant hope for our relationship. Our differences only widened our disconnection over time as we lived totally separate lives. Ben, to his credit, would still make an effort, inviting me to visit him, invitations I systematically spurned. I didn't see the value.

> **Conquering Mount Kilimanjaro is a physically and emotionally exhausting feat but the enduring summit paled in the feeling of shared accomplishment in our reunion, the restoration of our brotherly bond.**

Of course, my travels would change my perspective on a lot of things including how I connected with my brother. So when Ben told me about the trip he was planning the summer after his college graduation, I understood it for the priceless opportunity it was. Our trip to Las Vegas for a music festival would be the first we'd take together without the rest of our family, a weekend that changed the trajectory of our relationship. We promised to plan another trip soon.

It wasn't long that we found ourselves together on the roof of Africa. Conquering Mount Kilimanjaro is a physically and emotionally exhausting feat but the enduring summit paled in the feeling of shared accomplishment in our reunion, the restoration of our brotherly bond. Just like that, we were talking about girls, our experiences in college, along with our most intimate hopes and fears. The more we connected, I could only think of one thing—how proud I was of my little brother.

FROM TOP TO BOTTOM:

Summit day on Machame Route - Mount Kilimanjaro

Uhuru Peak - Mount Kilimanjaro

Bus Ticket to Karatu

Tanzania Visa

FROM TOP TO BOTTOM:

Jambiani - Zanzibar

Ngorongoro Conservation Area - Crater Highlands

FULL SPREAD:

Mount Kilimanjaro

TANZANIA

Tanzania

FROM LEFT TO RIGHT:

Maasai Mara National Reserve - Narok County

OPPOSITE PAGE:

Teenagers show off their best moves jumping into the water at Forodhoni Gardens in Stone Town, Zanzibar.

Maasai Mara Pass

All sorts of Obama branded products are available

BELOW & OPPOSITE PAGE:

Maasai Mara National Reserve - Narok County

Bwindi NP Stamp

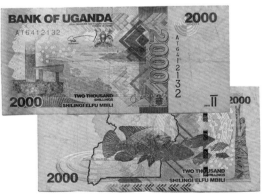

Uganda Shilling

ABOVE & FULL SPREAD:

The Bitukura group of gorillas in Bwindi Impenetrable Forest. You're told that the gorillas won't get within a dozen feet of you. Unfamiliar with such arbitrary regulations, one infant gorilla brazenly walked up right next to us, without hesitation, and began pounding his chest. Show off.

FROM LEFT TO RIGHT:

Ssese Islands - Lake Victoria - Kalangala District

Jinja

Rwandan Franc

Bus Ticket to Kigali

FROM LEFT TO RIGHT:

Nyungwe Forest Lodge Tea Hills

Nyungwe Rainforest

ETHIOPIA

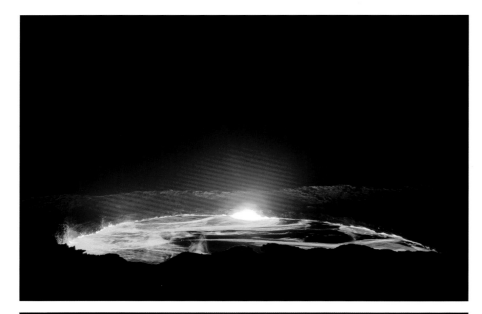

FROM TOP TO BOTTOM & FULL SPREAD:

The Danakil Depression in the Afar region is one of the hottest places on earth with an average year round temperature of 93 degrees fahrenheit (32 °C). The volcano located here, Erta Ale, is one of six active volcanoes with a lava lake currently in existence. On the right, miners transport salt slabs via camel caravans.

BELOW:

Goats in Mek'ele get strapped in for what will presumably be a terribly bumpy ride.

BOTTOM:

Simien Mountains Trekking – Ethiopian Highlands

BELOW:

In Harar, farmers began feeding wild hyenas raw meat as a daily ritual around the 1960s. Once full, they tend to leave the livestock alone. Not for the faint of heart.

BELOW:

Gelada monkeys are found only in the Ethiopian highlands. Unlike New York's pigeons, they've gotten so used to humans that they'll happily cuddle up next to you.

ABOVE:

Under its Coptic calendar, Ethiopia adds an additional thirteenth month of five or six additional days. You'll notice this newspaper was printed in 2006 (even though it was 2014). Even time is kept differently. Instead of placing the start of the day at midnight, Ethiopian time begins at dawn. 12pm East African time becomes 6am in Ethiopia.

LEFT:

House of Golgotha Mikael - Rock Hewn Churches of Lalibela

NEXT PAGE:

Church of St. George - Rock Hewn Churches of Lalibela

Ghanian Cedi

Ghana to Burkina Bus Ticket

LEFT:

The Kane Kwei Carpentry Workshop in Accra originated the concept of a "fantasy" coffin. Their latest project honors the deceased, who really loved soda.

BURKINA FASO

Visa Stamps from West Africa

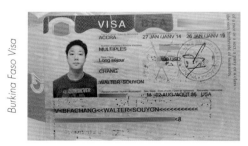

Burkina Faso Visa

FROM LEFT TO RIGHT:

Laongo Sculpture Symposium - Ouagadougou - Kadiogo Province

Village Artisanal - Ouagadougou - Kadiogo Province

CLOCKWISE, FROM RIGHT:

The sprawling Grand Marché de Dantokpain in Cotonou, Benin is the largest market in West Africa. The festish section is where animal skulls and skins are sold for traditional rituals.

TOGO

West Africa CFA Franc

Visa Entente for West Africa

Bus Ticket from Burkina Faso to Benin

RIGHT:

Lomé Beach - Lomé - Maritime Region

FROM LEFT TO RIGHT:

St. Paul's Cathedral - Abidjan

Giant snails in Abidjan Market

FROM LEFT TO RIGHT & FULL SPREAD:

Carnival - Olinda & Salvador

That's Felix. We met during Carnival, at a local restaurant near where I was staying in Salvador. Something about me brought him immense amusement and he insisted that we take a photo together, during which he couldn't stop beaming. As we posed, suddenly, he stopped us, and started to strip down into his underwear, which made me a little nervous at first. Until he proceeded to dress me up with costume. He even called his wife across the street who poked her head out the window to hear his excitement. Felix, now that was one happy man.

FROM LEFT TO RIGHT:

Praia da Atalaia - Fernando de Noronha - Pernambuco

Praia do Cachorro - Fernando de Noronha - Pernambuco

FROM TOP TO BOTTOM:

Largo do Pelourinho - Salvador - Bahia

Praia Mole - Florianópolis - Santa Catarina

VENEZUELA

Venezuelan Bolivar

Venezuela Visa Stamp

CLOCKWISE, FROM TOP LEFT:

Mount Roraima - Gran Sabana side

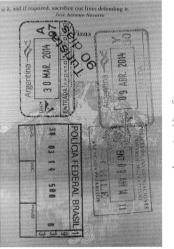

Argentina Visa Stamps

FROM LEFT TO RIGHT:

Iguazú Falls National Park

CHILE

CLOCKWISE, FROM TOP LEFT:

Santiago

Valparaíso

San Pedro de Atacama - Antofagasta Region

TOP:

Huacachina - Ica Region

BOTTOM ROW:

Santa Cruz Trek - Cordillera Blanca Range

ABOVE:

Salkantay Trek Trail

FULL SPREAD:

Machu Picchu - Cusco Region

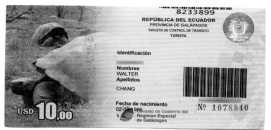

Island Tourist Tax

TOP LEFT:

Isabela Island

BOTTOM ROW:

Santa Cruz Island

OPPOSITE PAGE, FROM LEFT TO RIGHT:

Maras Salt Ponds - Sacred Valley of the Incas - Cusco Region

Moray Archaeological Site - Cusco Region

Entrance Ticket

CLOCKWISE, FROM RIGHT:

Parasolvent by Dan Benedict

Embrace by The Pier Group

Minaret by Bryan Tedrick

FULL SPREAD:

Zymphonic Wormhole by J-Kat and Shelly

CROATIA

CLOCKWISE, FROM TOP LEFT:

Split - Dalmatia Region

Plitvice Lakes NP - Lika-Senj County

Dubrovnik - Dalmatia Region

Westvleteren 12 Cap

Train ticket - Boom to Ghent

CLOCKWISE, FROM TOP RIGHT:

Ghent Canals - Flemish Region

Grand' Place-Grote Markt - Brussels

City Centre - Ghent - Flemish Region

NETHERLANDS

ABOVE:

Erasmus Bridge - Rotterdam - South Holland

TOP LEFT & BOTTOM LEFT:

Hacker-Pschorr Tent - Oktoberfest - Munich - Bavaria

Brandenburg Gate - Berlin

TOP RIGHT & BOTTOM RIGHT:

Festival of Lights - Berlin

Berlin Wall - Berlin

SWITZERLAND

CLOCKWISE, FROM TOP LEFT:

Mount Titlis Ski Resort - Engleberg

Matterhorn - Zermatt

Chapel Bridge - Lucerne

ABOVE:

View from top of City Hall - Lviv

RUSSIA

ABOVE:

Hermitage Museum - Saint Petersburg

Lantern Release Ticket

New Taiwan Dollar

FROM LEFT TO RIGHT:

Taipei 101 - Taipei

Jiufen - Ruifang District

BELARUS

While beautiful landscapes and ancient structures are often the focal points of travel, it's often the people you meet who leave the greatest impression on you. As I was backpacking solo, I often got asked the same question: Don't you ever get lonely?

But with the consistent flow of new people rotating in and out of my life daily, loneliness was never an issue. For the most part, I shared an experience with a person or a group of people and then we would split ways. Never to be seen or heard from again. But occasionally contact information was exchanged and we'd keep in touch. As my travels progressed I visited a handful of these new friends back in their own countries.

While I still keep in touch with several people online, the distance makes it difficult to maintain any sort of regular communication. Over time the sporadic online chatter simply grinds to a halt. However, there's one encounter that turned out to be something special.

I was eating dinner at a hostel in Samarkand, Uzbekistan, making conversation with a couple, when Nadia, a girl from Belarus, sat down at the table next to me and joined us. The couple eventually left but Nadia stayed and for the next five hours, we just talked, eventually taking a stroll around the city. I've always been a little awkward in these kinds of situations but with Nadia, everything felt effortless. We could talk about anything. I couldn't get enough, mesmerized by her stunning green eyes, her innocent expressions, but most of all, her infectious laugh. Even her voice, the sound, pace, and intonation of words were perfect to me. With Nadia, I felt natural being just totally silly. We'd known each other for a few hours, but as cliche as it sounds, I felt like I'd known her for years.

> " **I'd been a little anxious about meeting again after so long. What if it wasn't the same?** "

She left the next day. We said goodbye and then invited each other to come visit our respective countries in the future, per usual. I was a little sad, but I played it cool. She was moving to South Korea for work and I briefly thought about visiting her, but nothing came of it. I didn't want to set myself up for disappointment.

At first we conversed online. She had this way of communicating that was so earnest and straightforward. I was hooked. As we got to know each other better I kept telling myself it would fizzle out slowly. But the first few weeks turned into months and those months turned into a year.

Then in a moment of spontaneity, she flew out to New York while I was there for a weeklong stopover. Seeing her again, standing in front of me in Grand Central Station was a bit surreal. I had to pinch myself. I'd been anxious about meeting again after so long. What if it wasn't the same? But we clicked again instantly. Being together felt so right. It was perfect.

Since New York we've been to a handful of countries together, including Belarus, a country I never planned to visit or even knew existed until I met her. Will we last? I don't know. What I do know, after having traveled, is that I'm going to enjoy our journey.

Gomel Bus Ticket

Gomel to Minsk Train Ticket

BACKER SUPPORT

This book would have never been possible without the unbelievable support of the following people:

Nadzeya Shutava
Haryn Cho
Dan Yang
Jessica L. Ho
Susan Zheng
Derrick Weng
Craig Schlumpf
Alexandra Lam
Bill Sheehan
Franchesca Hwang
Kai Okamura
Anna Kim
Yargnawh
Thomas McCarvel
Arnaud De Fernando
Jung Choi
Elisha Hwang
Varun Shetty
Emily Cao
Ben Reid
Florian Kock
Shom Ghosh
Kong Chay-Ying
Jennifer Lee
Robert Blue
Sue Kim
Jae J. Yoon
Alex Kim
Minsung Cho
Aji C Pillai
Jessie & JR
Farid Kojima-san
Alec Liu
Daniel Nicoll
Julian Dahl
Michael Buonaiuto
Smith Won
Ninianne Alexis Bagtas
Melissa Guieb
Thel Hla
Dan Bandel Photography
Yuki Toyokawa
Ahmad Al-Benali
Mark DeCapua
Kim & Kris Bartell
Wendy Ko
Wenbo Shan
Tsvetelina Yordanova
Erika Choi
Christie Choi
Louis Choi
Joyce H. Lee
Andrew Chang
Gavin Scott
Arsène von Wyss

Andy Ukon
Jeong, Min, Isaac
& Casey Kim
Jordan W. Booth
Michael Fung
Patrick HM Chan
Bob Bursick
Elodie Amblard
Andrew McDonell
Carlo M. Ciaramelletti
JM Caracci
Mariana Abusada
Owen Kim
Linda S. Zhang
Laurence Crumbie
Jonathan Flynn
Noel Nixdorf
Reinhart
Carola Bertone
Jae M Hwang
Sammy Kim
The Um Family
Joshua Hird
Radu MP
Rose & Wayne
Melissa Lee
Robert Schulman
Divan Divanov
Robert Xu
David Manning
Brian Doll
Magnus von Koeller
Jaime Macias
Scott Klender
Lisa Johnson
R5
Hans Verfaillie
Doucet Joris
Rogel Sokolin-Maimon
Austin & Edie Cooper
Christoph Meade
Katherine Larson
Leon Selby
Shivani Grover
Sawetpatama
Ssebudde Ibrahim
Wooyeon Park
Nuri
Anita Phagan
Jennifer English
Connor Jordan
Dave Clifford
Hoe Jung
Shyam Amin
Digvijay Singh

Danvy Antoine
Ricky Long
Sacha Brady
Jonas Michalko Hamann
Philip Shepherd
Warren Stevens
Bong-hee Yang
Sung Yang
Alan Kong
Theodore James Barrett
Madeline Shortt
Kyle Crichton
Joosup Lim
Jonathan Yang
Brice Wong-Tze-Kioon
Roger Keller
Dion den Hollander
Corinna Vigier
Aurélien Blachet
Sandy Lee
Marc Hedlund
Ricky & Irene Moy
Francesca Manea
Jaime
Jang Moon Hee
Wonil Ryu
Haein Son
Ying Zhu
Nino Rajic
Marcel Uekermann
Gena Lew Gong
Empress Jinnie
Tracy Lauren Jaico
Alexis Chalumeau
Kevin Schumacher
Kevin Chuang
Gregory Pachacz
Pacharapol Adulavidhaya
Brian MacDuckston
Christien Vanherck
Illmari Pekonen
Elaine Mantinan
Darlene G Wade
Christine Cho
Jazreel Hong
Shuo Li
Jake Karpieszuk
Markus Leimbach
Alison Grasso
Orin Saunders
Nick Goedeke
Tara Russell
Dhruv Amin
Jennifer Dzieniszewski
Patrick Quaedackers

Kristy Carstairs
Sophia Lim
Mavis Hee
Michael Ted-Wing Li
Christian Wenz
Marica Barezzani
Justin Parsons
Sheyla Gomes Castillo
Daniel Koren
Thomas Ally
Sarita Hedge Roy
My-Dao Huynh
Krisztina Rozsos
Matthew Lin Shaolong
Khanh Nguyen
Holley Arbeit
Jason Bogdanski
Andrew Yancey
Angela Tien-Hui Lai
Davide Marano
Roberto Loar
Kenji Butler
Christine H. Kim
Patrick Jones
Lizzie Tang
Matt & Becca Rawlins
Caroline Pahl
Kelly Lissolo
Gyuwon Anthony Cha
Susan Liu
Wonchul Ryu
Sookhee Chang
Wootae Yoo
Yeoh Phee Lee
Ryan
Nihat Sinan Erül
Kan Wang
Jose Armando Villagomez-Rivadeneyra
Andrea Mainardi
Tobias Löhe
Steve Kuebelbeck
Barry Ford
Cristiano Medeiros Dalbem
Benoit
Kaushlesh Biyani
Biyani Photography
Jason Chan
Claudio Reggiani
Kara M.
Dave Carden
Jason Park
Teo Wei Ren & Fiona Pang
Paul Paluch
Tom Fritz Loest

Anna Karaulova
Cern Basher
Andrew "Chim" Beckwith
Tony Fon
Linh Tran
Pawel Dmytrow
Emma Armstrong
Pasakorn Sangsak
Nicole Kalisz
Kai and Charmaine
Aram Balakjian
Bernd Spörl
Jules Bossert
Bill Lam
Darryl Kang
Markus Laile
Wai
Jean Timken
Boyd H Kaneshiro
Ken Hui
Christian Huber
Francesco Bassanelli
Jenna Ahlborn
Johnnie Ngoon
Wooyeong Kim
Wendy Lai
Michael Lee
John Vu
Voor Flo, liefs Joost en Suus
Jessica Chue
Cris Luetto
Leo Chien
Carol Drewes
Carson Kolberg
D.A. Hughes & Associates
Holger Looks
Abby Chandler
Sharon Cunningham
Trent Nakamura
Eric Rosenberg
Jörg Deeters
Christian Börner
Geert Valk
Christopher Chan
The LEO Book
Fetz Othmar
Pai Hwong
Blaž Štefe
Adam Moore
Michael Bracey
Lisa H. Tai
Bob Weinstein
Mick and Susan Wagoner
Nicolas Carrier
Philip Pachacz

Craig Wong
Vinorthan Joseph
Matt Hudson
Edwin Chan
Kaci Risser
John-Peter Widmer
Amalia Marin
Mr. Angus Ho
Max Lin
Jack Chong
Ji Yoo
atomicbee.cz
Loic Etienne
Tony
Karl Lee
Daniel Weng
Courtney Kronenberger
Vivian Yunge An
Ted Szeto & Angela Tseng
Harry Martin-Dreyer
Pierluigi Bullo
John Easton
Marvin Bindemann
Larry Susman
Brandon Eversole
Matteo Berchier
Barac Mădălin Cristian
Betty Yan
Jennifer Campbell
Alan Nicolás Becker Capuyá
Oliver Finch
Keith Angela Maya Riley - Hoisington
Pornthep Pisalangkul
Brett Rogers
Franziska Maeder
Sandra Dillon
Soufong Chan
Carlos Romero
Katrina Maniku
Eric Jeker
Mario Aquaro
Luis Gino Prada Guzman
Marco Rosales Jr.
Vicrooloo
Kathy Henderson
A K Cox
Doug Kea
Justina Chow
Margit M.
Brendan Meier
theredphone
Troy Lewis Kasemodel
Nelson Ray
Sharat Faqurudheen

theredphone
Troy Lewis Kasemodel
Nelson Ray
Sharat Faqurudheen
Jeroen Rouers
Shabbir M
Daniel G Weese
John Agostini
Dr. Bonifaz Kaufmann
Cath Cuisson
Viktor Dreger
Tasha Pang
Neal Mody
@charizze
David Garrido Martínez
Jesse Lee
Jonathan Hsieh
Scott Graham
Edgar Ayala
Danny Cantu
Alvin Fong
Marcus Yeo Chueng Kiat
Sella Peled
Joo Won Park
Kristy Tipton
Guido Agapito
Robert Brennan
Shaye Khalid
Keenan Alexandre Brown
Elisa Maselli
Stephen Huggins
Dennis d Brennan
Filippo
Blaesing Thompson Family
Cecille Espiritu
Armond Netherly
Bob Cason
David Portillo
Vicki Huang
Ole-Morten Larsen
Jenny Xuan
Amanda Keele
Jisang Park
Christopher Dolan
Diego Hernando Loeda
Emily Dorsa
Jason Marlin
Doc PuD
Jos van Baal
Zoe Martin
LOR Vincent
Trent Mitchell
Duarte Pinheiro
Chris Banks - For Kristy
Thiago Norio Yoshida

Trent Mitchell
Duarte Pinheiro
Chris Banks - For Kristy
Thiago Norio Yoshida
Nora Neo-Crothers
Chelsea Giles-Hansen
Stefan Jouaux
Valentin Abaluta
Sandeep
Clara CN Chow
Kristi Swanson
Sebastian Stach
Cory Adair
Lily Ko
Hillel Koren
Ray Cho
Hannah
Antu Nehuen
Melissa Lee
Greg Avedesian
Elisha Hwang
Andy Yukon
Olivier Monnier
Natan Giuliano
Anthony Kontekakis
Flora Pereira da Silva
Daniel Unger
Ryan James Terribilini
George Castro
Evan Wojtanek
Daniel Nicoll
Harshil Shah
Mara Cantonao
Regis Frias
Norman Yahya
Firat
Surayya
Mohamed Sadek
Nader Mores
Taylor Murphy
Oh Jarucha Janmekha
Bridget Hardy
Ring Jo
Jonghyun Hyun
Anna Engle
Fahad Azad
Ted Lackman
Klaus Bochmann
Laurence Crumbie
Dmytro Kudlinskyi
Sebastiaan van den Broek
Konstantinos Malliotakis
Ghassab Ai-Bedoul
Fabiola Hwang
Thiago Norio Yoshida
Konstantinos Malliotakis

Wagner da Rosa
Ghassab Ai-Bedoul
Fabiola Hwang
Wagner da Rosa
Arthur Oliveira
Igor Amorim
Edem Dzidzienyo
Patrick Fisher
Hernan Sanchez
Glade
Shana Rogers
Lari
Xavier Allard
Francesca Manea
Sarah Donvito
Lila Neiswanger
Chay Ying Kong
Pim Logie
Moe
Lena
Beau Lynn Miller
Edson Walker
Steve Rhy

153

COUNTRY LIST

Argentina	Israel	South Korea
Australia	Japan	Taiwan
Belarus	Jordan	Switzerland
Belgium	Kenya	Tajikistan
Benin	Kyrgyzstan	Tanzania
Bolivia	Lesotho	Thailand
Brazil	Malaysia	Turkey
Burkina Faso	Mexico	Togo
Cambodia	Myanmar	Uganda
Côte d'Ivoire	Mozambique	Ukraine
Chile	Namibia	United Arab Emirates
China	Nepal	United States of America
Colombia	Netherlands	Uzbekistan
Croatia	New Zealand	Vietnam
Cuba	North Korea	Venezuela
Ecuador	Oman	Zimbabwe
Egypt	Palau	
Ethiopia	Peru	
Germany	Philippines	
Greece	Russia	
Ghana	Rwanda	
India	Singapore	
Indonesia	South Africa	

157

158